THE
#DEAR
WORSHIP
LEADER

HANDBOOK

65 TWEETS
THAT WILL REVOLUTIONIZE
YOUR WORSHIP LEADING

The author has taken reasonable precautions in the preparation of this book and believes the facts presented in the book are accurate as of the date it was written. The author specifically disclaims any liability resulting from the use or application of the information contained in this book, and the information is not intended to serve as legal, financial, or other professional advice related to individual situations.

Editorial Consulting By Farrah Nicole Martin, MPH, MAEd

Published By:
Jasher Press & Co.
Email: jasherpress@gmail.com
Contact Number: 252.571.3874
New Bern, NC 28562

TWEETS

Tweet 1: #DearWorshipLeader you may have to do it for free long before you get to do it for a fee. Be faithful either way.

Tweet 2: #DearWorshipLeader do not do this for money. Because once you have it, your worship will never be the same.

Tweet 3: #DearWorshipLeader sing with the lyrics not over them. The words to the song are more important than your vocals.

Tweet 4: #DearWorshipLeader practice. Then practice some more. And then practice again.

Tweet 5: #DearWorshipLeader dead space between songs is not good. Fill it with praise.

Tweet 6: #DearWorshipLeader pride will kill you. Sing background vocals sometimes just to remind yourself that it is not about you.

Tweet 7: #DearWorshipLeader find out who wrote the song and send them a thank you. Without them, you would not sound as good. And they will appreciate it.

Tweet 8: #DearWorshipLeader learn how to end the song. You'll get them on the next one.

Tweet 9: #DearWorshipLeader study other worship leaders. You cannot lead if you cannot learn.

Tweet 10: #DearWorshipLeader an uninhibited praise will release an uninhibited blessing. So do not be cute.

Tweet 11: #DearWorshipLeader not only can they hear your voice they can see your face. So smile. It's called a "joyful" noise!

Tweet 12: #DearWorshipLeader people are watching your worship when you are not on stage. Bring the same fire from the floor as you do when you are in front.

Tweet 13: #DearWorshipLeader do not let the size of the crowd dictate the size of your energy. Every service deserves the same focus.

Tweet 14: #DearWorshipLeader It's called a mic not a knife. Fight your enemies another time. Don't work out your rage from the stage.

Tweet 15: #DearWorshipLeader you must see the crowd and the clock. Don't go over board by going over time.

Tweet 16: #DearWorshipLeader the congregation is the choir. Teach them to sing along so you don't have to sing alone.

Tweet 17: #DearWorshipLeader What you wear matters. If it don't fit, you must relent. People are easily distracted.

Tweet 18: #DearWorshipLeader if it doesn't excite you it won't excite them. Learn to love the song your singing.

Tweet 19: #DearWorshipLeader if they need musical training to sing it then it's probably too complicated. Simple always wins.

Tweet 20: #DearWorshipLeader you may have to sing another song. So always have an extra on hand and ready to go.

Tweet 21: #DearWorshipLeader if you keep trying to "kill the room" you will end up killing your voice. Flow with the spirit and let the song dictate the delivery.

Tweet 22: #DearWorshipLeader if the song is not right, put it to flight. Save it for another day.

Tweet 23: #DearWorshipLeader its going to sound strange if it's not in your range. Let someone else sing it.

Tweet 24: #DearWorshipLeader the anointing will cost you something. Sometimes the sacrifice of praise will cost you the sacrifice of pleasure.

Tweet 25: #DearWorshipLeader there is a difference between singing the song and releasing the sound. You must do both.

Tweet 26: #DearWorshipLeader it is going to be difficult to do in public what you have never done in private. Don't just be a worship leader be a worshipper.

Tweet 27: #DearWorshipLeader if you can stand for the singing you can sit for the sermon. You need a word too.

Tweet 28: #DearWorshipLeader God loves you. Let that be enough.

Tweet 29: #DearWorshipLeader if you can't move God then you can't move the people. Sing to impress Him not them.

Tweet 30: #DearWorshipLeader never get so caught up with the title that you lose sight of the throne. It's His Kingdom, not yours.

Tweet 31: #DearWorshipLeader the crowd may not respond the way you want them to. Worship anyway.

Tweet 32: #DearWorshipLeader if you can't fall at his feet you can't receive from His hand.

Tweet 33: #DearWorshipLeader if you abuse the position you will lose the platform. Keep yourself in check.

Tweet 34: #DearWorshipLeader always point the attention back to Him. You're a guide not a God. Make sure that's extremely clear.

Tweet 35: #DearWorshipLeader don't rebuke the devil more than you reverence God. Satan is under your feet. The Savior is above your head. Look Up!

Tweet 36: #DearWorshipLeader never mistake their applause for Him as applause for you. Stay in your lane.

Tweet 37: #DearWorshipLeader if you only give a praise offering and never a financial offering you are robbing yourself of major blessings.

Tweet 38: #DearWorshipLeader you send the wrong message when you give a church your talent but not your tithe. There cannot be true worship without a true sacrifice.

Tweet 39: #DearWorshipLeader if you can't honor the church you don't deserve an honorarium.

Tweet 40: #DearWorshipLeader they may forget your check. Forgive them. And bring the fire anyway.

Tweet 41: #DearWorshipLeader the congregation can fall out but you can't. You cannot lead them if you leave them staring at an empty stage.

Tweet 42: #DearWorshipLeader do not yell at the congregation. You are not their shepherd.

Tweet 43: #DearWorshipLeader if you show them they'll follow. If you shout at them they'll falter. Be the model not the monster.

Tweet 44: #DearWorshipLeader just because you are anointed doesn't mean you're administrative. Find a volunteer who can help you.

Tweet 45: #DearWorshipLeader they need your set list well in advance. You and God can't be the only ones with the songs.

Tweet 46: #DearWorshipLeader the sound engineer is your friend. Treat them well and they will help you. Treat them wrong and they will mess with your microphone.

Tweet 47: #DearWorshipLeader be nice to the band. You are going to need them to cover you at some point.

Tweet 48: #DearWorshipLeader if you don't correct it, it'll get out of control. If you don't confront it, it won't change. Your team is longing for your leadership.

Tweet 49: #DearWorshipLeader every now and then do something fun with your volunteers. Let them see that you're not a super hero all the time!

Tweet 50: #DearWorshipLeader defend your team and they'll defend you. Expose them and they'll expose you.

Tweet 51: #DearWorshipLeader your team will listen to what you say but they will imitate what you do. Never demand what you do not demonstrate.

Tweet 52: #DearWorshipLeader don't cuff the mic. The sound engineer hates it and we don't hear you that clearly.

Tweet 53: #DearWorshipLeader if you don't use your monitor you will lose your mind and your voice. Do a sound check.

Tweet 54: #DearWorshipLeader end rehearsal on time. Your team will thank you.

Tweet 55: #DearWorshipLeader if you don't know the lyrics neither will your team. They are a reflection of your work habits.

Tweet 56: #DearWorshipLeader you must learn the art of singing and signaling. Don't lead the crowd and lose the band.

Tweet 57: #DearWorshipLeader you must know a hymn. Yes, they are old. But, they're still gold. Always have one ready.

Tweet 58: #DearWorshipLeader learn how to sing with flashing lights and fog machines. They aren't going anywhere. So embrace it.

Tweet 59: #DearWorshipLeader you must be able to lead worship in different styles of music. If you can only sing in one genre, you will only reach one group.

Tweet 60: #DearWorshipLeader if you can't stand the pastor please don't stand in their pulpit. There's just too much pollution in that praise.

Tweet 61: #DearWorshipLeader sing more, talk less. There is a sermon coming after you.

Tweet 62: #DearWorshipLeader if the senior pastor doesn't like it, then don't do it. If you won't follow their lead, you won't follow God's either.

Tweet 63: #DearWorshipLeader sometimes our season is up. Embrace it. God has so much more in store for us.

Tweet 64: #DearWorshipLeader you must train someone younger to do what you do. Your Pastor and your church will thank you!

Tweet 65: #DearWorshipLeader this is not a competition. If God called you then He qualified you. So just be you!

INTRODUCTION

I remember the first time I led worship for my church. It was a hot summer day in August. I was standing in my normal spot on stage with the rest of the tenors in the choir. The room felt electric. The spirit was high. The worship was on fire. The entire church seemed to be orbiting into Heaven.

All of a sudden I noticed our worship pastor was having trouble singing. We were on our third service of the day and I knew she had been fighting a cold since the day before. It seemed as if her voice began to fade. The longer the song went the weaker her voice got.

Without any warning she turned, threw me the microphone, and walked toward the side of the stage. Like a wide receiver catching a pass from a quarterback, I took that microphone and ran with it. That's not a figure of speech. I literally ran with the microphone.

I ran to the right side of the stage, dancing, jumping, and sliding around. Then I ran to the left side of the stage, spinning, shaking, and sliding around again.

I was on Cloud 9! I was living out a childhood dream. I knew I was in my calling. I knew I had embarked on the very thing I was created to do.

That was my first day as a worship leader. Since that day I have experienced the highs, and the lows of being a worship leader. I have done some things very well, and I have made some critical mistakes.

11

I have had moments that I want to remember forever, and I have had moments that I never want to remember again. All in all I have learned so many lessons and gained so much wisdom over the past 10+ years of worship leading.

I wrote this book to help worship leaders excel in their development, and avoid the mistakes that I've made along the way.

This is the book I wish I had when I started out as a worship leader. These are the lessons I wish someone had prepared me for when I first got started.

So many worship leaders are under pressure. They feel the pressure of having to create a great worship environment, build a solid team, support their Pastors vision, and honor their church.

They feel the pressure of having to choose the right songs every week, wear the right clothes that people will like, and maintain the right image that will represent the church well.

They often feel like they are overworked, underpaid, understaffed, and sometimes unappreciated.

In spite of these pressures we are driven by a higher call. We are compelled to do this week in and week out. To not do it would go against our spiritual instinct, our purpose, and our mission.

I wrote this book to help worship leaders as well as pastors. Most of the lessons I share in this book were taught to me in the offices of the Senior Pastors I have served over the years.

I have been challenged, corrected, and educated by a Senior Pastor in each of the areas I share in this book.

All of the principles may not apply to your specific church. Every church is different. But all of the principles will convey the spirit and heart behind the position of a worship leader.

Do not feel as if you have to read this book all at one time in one sitting. It is ok to jump around, or apply one tweet before moving on to the next.

The #DearWorshipLeader Handbook is guaranteed to revolutionize your worship leading. This book promises to sharpen you, strengthen you, and stretch you.

Some tweets may be easier to digest than others. Some may downright offend you. But they were all written with love for your growth.

I pray that as you embark on this journey that God would give you wisdom, divine favor, and an abundance of peace.

God Bless You,

Brian M. Bullock

TWEET 1

#DEARWORSHIPLEADER YOU MAY HAVE TO DO IT FOR FREE LONG BEFORE YOU GET TO DO IT FOR A FEE. BE FAITHFUL EITHER WAY.

Picture this- a young person alone in their bedroom, an upside down hairbrush in their hand and an audience of gazing toys and stuffed animals intently focused on the budding singer in front of them. Sound familiar? Many of today's worship leaders began singing in this exact posture long before they ever stepped foot on a stage in front of a crowd. This child was not worshipping in their bedroom for money. As worship leaders, we step into these shoes because of our love for God and our passion to see His people enter into His presence. Whether you receive compensation from your church or not, keep your motives pure. Remind yourself daily why you do this. What we do is not for fame or fortune, but instead to make the name of Jesus the most exalted name on the earth.

#DEARWORSHIPLEADER DO NOT DO THIS FOR MONEY. BECAUSE ONCE YOU HAVE IT, YOUR WORSHIP WILL NEVER BE THE SAME.

Money is a great servant, but a horrible master. If you are leading just for the money, it will come out. You cannot fake passion. People can tell when you are sincere and genuine about what you are doing. The pastor can tell if this is a job to you or a calling that must be fulfilled in your life. I believe in honoring worship leaders with a financial blessing. I think it is awesome to be able to attend a church where they value the position of worship leader so much they are willing to give a full time salary for it. However, there is a difference between a worship leader who is paid and a worship leader who only wants to be paid. The motives are different. The heart behind those two things are not the same. Be a worship leader because you love to serve. Do it because doing anything else would leave you feeling empty. Be a worship leader because getting people to Jesus is the most important thing in your life. And if money chases you in the process, then thank God. If you go chasing it, though, you will lose the purity and passion you had when you were first called.

TWEET 3

#DEARWORSHIPLEADER SING WITH THE LYRICS NOT OVER THEM. THE WORDS TO THE SONG ARE MORE IMPORTANT THAN YOUR VOCALS.

Sometimes worship leaders treat their set like an audition for "The Voice." There are so many vocal acrobatics that it feels like you're watching a "singing gymnastics" competition at the Olympics rather than participating in a time of worship to God. People love the runs and may be amazed by vocal range and skill, but above all else, they really want an encounter with Christ. A worship leader's vocal ability can enhance the lyrics of the song, but should not draw attention away from them. Let the words minister to the hearts of the congregation. This will have more impact and lessen the amount of energy needed to create a moment of worship. There is a grace that comes when we step out of self-effort and allow the Spirit to move through the lyrics and among the people.

TWEET 4

#DEARWORSHIPLEADER PRACTICE. THEN PRACTICE SOME MORE. AND THEN PRACTICE AGAIN.

One of my mentors has a saying that practice does not make perfect, it makes permanent. If you do not practice well you will not present well. The greatest worship leaders practice constantly. They rehearse the songs, they go over their signals, they work on their techniques, and they envision the finished moment. You cannot rely solely on gifting, or anointing. You must add a strong work ethic to what God has invested in you. The congregation can tell when you have not practiced. Your church can feel when you are free-styling and piecing things together at the last minute. The band knows it and your singers know it. Be prepared to lead people into worship. Practice until everything you need to know and do is permanently imprinted in your heart.

TWEET 5

#DEARWORSHIPLEADER DEAD SPACE BETWEEN SONGS IS NOT GOOD. FILL IT WITH PRAISE.

There are few things more awkward than ending a song and waiting for the next one to begin. That small space in between songs can feel like an eternity. If you had not planned exactly what the transition will be and how it will go, you can end up standing on stage looking around as if you lost your house keys. That brief moment of dead silence can be a huge distraction and can stagnate the momentum in your set. Work with the band to ensure that there is no dead space. Practice your transitions with them. And if all else fails fill that space with praise. Not forceful, demanding praise, but a graceful and flowing praise that everyone can join. When everyone is singing a song to the Lord or shouting out a praise in unison it creates a beautiful sound. Unless you are strategically silencing the room because of the presence of God, fill that dead space and rehearse your transitions.

TWEET 6

#DEARWORSHIPLEADER PRIDE WILL KILL YOU. SING BACKGROUND VOCALS SOMETIMES JUST TO REMIND YOURSELF THAT IT IS NOT ABOUT YOU.

Leading people in worship can give you a powerful feeling. With one command you can have an entire room of people lifting their hands or raising their voices. It can give you a feeling of control and authority that you might not feel in any other area of your life. That is why every worship leader has to fight the spirit of pride. We are constantly in the front and always being told how great we are and celebrated for our singing ability. This is why it is crucial that we remain humble. After enough compliments, even the most confident and spiritual of people can start to rely on the affirmations given by the crowd. If you let pride creep in, it will contaminate your worship and set you up for a huge fall. Every now and then, let someone else lead. Sing in the background and watch the people be led by someone else. It will remind you that you are part of a team and not the center of attention. People come for an encounter with God. Whether it is you or someone else, they are looking for a worship leader that can help them encounter Jesus. Stay humble and never feed off the applause of people.

TWEET 7

#DEARWORSHIPLEADER FIND OUT WHO WROTE THE SONG AND SEND THEM A THANK YOU. WITHOUT THEM, YOU WOULD NOT SOUND AS GOOD. AND THEY WILL APPRECIATE IT.

Not every worship leader is a songwriter. And not every songwriter is a worship leader. As worship leaders, we owe songwriters a huge thank you. They write music that touch peoples' hearts and make us sound incredibly good. Without those songwriters, many of us would sound like cats in an alley- screeching and screaming with no melodic beauty associated with our sound. Thank God for those who have written songs that have become the anthems of our lives. We should appreciate all those who have contributed to a culture of worship spreading throughout this generation. Do not just cover a writer's songs; cover the person with prayer, appreciation, and support. Find out who has written your favorite songs and send them a message letting them know how much you appreciate their investment into the kingdom.

TWEET 8

#DEARWORSHIPLEADER LEARN HOW TO END THE SONG. YOU'LL GET THEM ON THE NEXT ONE.

Whenever my wife makes a great meal, I ask her this same question as I get towards the end of my plate, "Is there more?" We all want more of a good thing. Especially worship leaders. When we hit that high point in a song, where everything seems to be flowing and the spirit is moving, our instinct is to want more and more and more. So we reprise it, remix, rewrite it, and revise it again and again. We hate having to end a good song. We never want to leave on a high note. We want the song to last forever. Unfortunately, all good things must come to an end. You must be wise enough to know how to end a song. Sometimes the powerful moment was for a moment. Do not box God in to one verse or one chorus on a particular song. He can move just as much on the next song as He did on the last one. As hard as it may be, you must raise your right arm, close your right fist, look to the band, and tell them to end the song. It is ok to keep the congregation wanting more. It makes them want to see you again. It creates great energy and expectation the next time you sing that song. So never worry about moving to the next song. God is still in the room and He will still move on your behalf.

TWEET 9

#DEARWORSHIPLEADER STUDY OTHER WORSHIP LEADERS. YOU CANNOT LEAD IF YOU CANNOT LEARN.

When was the last time you talked to another worship leader about their experiences and asked questions looking to glean knowledge from them? When was the last time you raised your hands, lifted up your voice, and had an encounter with God while another worship leader was leading on stage? To be an effective leader you must also be a persistent student. You cannot just be a leader; be a learner. Seek wisdom and guidance from people who have been doing it longer than you have. Watch and admire the energy of those who are younger than you are. Recognize that you can learn something from every worship leader. In the same way we all have different DNA, we all have different worship styles. Each of us bring a unique approach to worship. Study everyone. Ask questions, take notes, and become a student. It would be a mistake to think that our style is the best style or the only style that matters. It is arrogance that causes us not to ask questions or consider gleaning information from someone else. Push past your discomfort and pursue the wisdom of your peers. It will increase your understanding and give you tools that will enhance what you already do. Do not be afraid to ask for advice. Do not hesitate to attend a worship conference. Connect with your peers so that you can grow into what God has called you.

TWEET 10

#DEARWORSHIPLEADER AN UNINHIBITED PRAISE WILL RELEASE AN UNINHIBITED BLESSING. SO DO NOT BE CUTE.

I must admit that I am a little biased towards this particular topic. Mainly because I do not look cute when I lead worship. When I worship, I am crying. I have my ugly face on, I am on the floor, and I am ripping my jacket. I admire worship leaders who have so much self-control and restraint when they worship that they never sweat, they have the perfect smile, and even their hair does not move one inch. I have not been able to conquer that just yet. However, I have learned that every now and then when you focus less on being cute and let yourself go, something powerful happens. It is as if an uninhibited praise opens up the door to uninhibited blessings. I have seen God do miraculous things when the worship became free and open. When the pastor looks at you and gives you the signal to keep going and not worry about the time, the whole room explodes because everyone knows that the Lord has shown up. This may not be your style or within your personality, but if you ever feel the need to cry when leading, it is ok to let the tears flow. It is ok to jump up and down. It is ok to dance and move to the rhythm of the music. Be appropriate for your setting, but be free. When you are free, the people who are worshipping with you will be free. And free worship ushers in the presence of God.

TWEET 11

#DEARWORSHIPLEADER NOT ONLY CAN THEY HEAR YOUR VOICE THEY CAN SEE YOUR FACE. SO SMILE. IT'S CALLED A "JOYFUL" NOISE!

The gospel is good news! Jesus is alive. He has risen from the dead. He now sits on the right hand of the Father and makes intercession for us. There was a day when people had to pay their own penalty for sin. The cost of that sin was death. Today we have access to God and forgiveness of our sins through Jesus. Rather than giving us the curse we deserve, He gives us the blessing that Christ earned on our behalf. This is great news and an incredibly important revelation. Why on earth would you want to communicate this gospel, about this God with a sad, depressing, and unenthused expression? Singing about the good news of Jesus with a melancholy face is like serving filet mignon from Ruth's Chris on a rusty, smelly garbage can lid. The two do not go together. I am not suggesting that you have a "Colgate smile" the entire time you are leading worship, but I am suggesting that you appear engaged and like you want to be there. People are not just hearing your voice they are seeing your face. Do not destroy with your body language what you are trying to create with your worship. Let every part of you get involved in the worship experience. Lift your hands, stomp your feet, and every now and then wear a smile so that your teeth can bless the Lord.

TWEET 12

#DEARWORSHIPLEADER PEOPLE ARE WATCHING YOUR WORSHIP WHEN YOU ARE NOT ON STAGE. BRING THE SAME FIRE FROM THE FLOOR AS YOU DO WHEN YOU ARE IN FRONT.

Imagine going to a public pool on a sizzling hot summer day. As you get closer to the pool, you realize that someone is in it and they appear to be drowning. You grab a pole or stick and help the drowning person out of the pool. They thank you for saving their life and tell you that the pool will be available in a few moments. They then proceed to put on a t-shirt that says lifeguard and make their way up the steps to the lifeguard chair. Then they tell you all is safe and you can now use the pool. If you are anything like me, you will head for the nearest exit and run as far away from that pool as possible. If the lifeguard cannot save himself, how can he save me? If what he is doing is not working for him, how am I to believe that it will work for me? You cannot be a worship leader who only worships when you have your "lifeguard" t-shirt on. I need to know that you can swim when you are not in your special chair. The congregation watches you when you are not on stage. They want to see do you really know how to "swim". They want to know that their worship leader loves to worship even when they are not on stage. You can do more to create a culture of worship in your church from the floor than you can from the stage. On the floor, you are a part of the congregation. You are among the people and adding your voice to the sea of voices worshipping God. There is power when you become part of the choir. Bring the fire from your seat. Yes, that time is private for you, but as a leader you are constantly inspiring others in their journey. Your worship inspires others to get into the pool!

TWEET 13

#DEARWORSHIPLEADER DO NOT LET THE SIZE OF THE CROWD DICTATE THE SIZE OF YOUR ENERGY. EVERY SERVICE DESERVES THE SAME FOCUS.

I have two children. I love them both dearly. They have two completely different personalities and energy levels. When I walk through the door, they both want my attention. They want me to play with them, talk with them, and watch television with them. Every time they see me they expect me to be energetic and ready to play. They do not care about my challenges. They are not interested in hearing about how things are going at work. They do not provide their shoulders for me to cry on. They want my attention to be on them and they want my energy to be the way it always is. They are looking for me to set the tone. I never let their energy determine my energy. I push myself, even when I am tired, to give them thirty minutes of unrelenting joy and connection. It is the same way as a worship leader. Whether it is an early morning service, a late evening service, an older congregation, or a younger audience, the people want you to bring your energy and passion to the worship experience. Be the fire starter. Be the one who gets the celebration in gear. Never be swayed by the audience. Especially the size of the audience. If you are only lively when the audience is big then you are not maximizing the gift that God has given to you. I have been in a room with just a few people but felt the presence of God so strong and heavy that it felt like a million people were in the room. Be energetic and passionate no matter what and God will honor the purity of your heart.

TWEET 14

#DEARWORSHIPLEADER IT'S CALLED A MIC NOT A KNIFE. FIGHT YOUR ENEMIES ANOTHER TIME. DON'T WORK OUT YOUR RAGE FROM THE STAGE.

If there is one thing I do not like, it is getting in trouble for something somebody else did. This happened to me often when I was in high school. We had a teacher named Mr. Corver. He was a retired war veteran who was very irritable and easily provoked. My classmates took great pleasure in agitating him. They loved to watch him "snap." One day somebody put a bunch of chalk in his cup of coffee while he was out of the classroom. When he returned to drink some of his hot morning brew, he soon realized he had sipped a medium coffee with two sugars and three chalk sticks! He was furious. He demanded to know who did it. No one would tell him. So in return he gave everyone a week's worth of detention. I personally did not like being punished for something I did not do. I felt that had he done a little more work he could have easily identified the kid who was laughing hysterically in the corner with chalk all over his shirt and hands. As a worship leader, do not punish the congregation for something one member did. Do not use the microphone to send subliminal messages to your haters. Never turn the platform into a boxing ring. It is a place for praise not for punching. This is why it is critical that you are singing to the Lord and about the Lord so that your focus will always be on Him. Then, your worship will be a blessing to everyone.

TWEET 15

#DEARWORSHIPLEADER YOU MUST SEE THE CROWD AND THE CLOCK. DON'T GO OVERBOARD BY GOING OVER TIME.

I am a huge football fan. Tom Brady is my favorite quarterback. I love to watch him play the game. I am always amazed at his ability to read the defense and make the appropriate play in a split second. He has this innate ability to see multiple things at one time. He sees the play clock, the receivers, the defense, and his offensive line protection. As a quarterback, he has to be precise and prepared. He has a little bit of time to do many different things. Worship leaders are the quarterbacks during worship. We must see everything that is happening in the room. We have to know where we are in the song, what song is next, whose part doesn't sound right, how much time do we have left, what is the Lord saying to us, what do the musicians need right now, and a plethora of other things. To be an effective worship leader you must be committed to excellence and efficiency. If they give you twenty minutes to worship then only take twenty minutes. If they give you an hour to worship then only take an hour. You must be skilled enough to know what is happening in the spirit and in the natural. You must be able to see Christ and the clock. The moment you go past your allotted time, you are operating outside of your authority. Be powerful, but also be professional.

TWEET 16

#DEARWORSHIPLEADER THE CONGREGATION IS THE CHOIR. TEACH THEM TO SING ALONG SO YOU DON'T HAVE TO SING ALONE.

Over the years, there are two main questions I have been asked in regards to worship. The first, "Why do we make people stand up the entire time worship is going on?" and the second "Why do worship songs repeat the same lyrics over and over and over?" Well, the reason we suggest people stand during the worship service is because we do not want worship to be a performance. We do not want it to turn into a concert. We are not inviting people to watch a choir sing, but rather we are inviting the congregation to be the choir that is singing. The congregation is the choir. There is nothing more powerful than hearing a room full of worshippers singing to heaven's throne. The reason why the songs are repetitive and simple is to help the average person sing along. The worship leader should not be singing alone. Our job is to help the congregation be the choir. Encourage them to not only watch, but to participate. Lead them into songs that declare the goodness of God and the magnitude of His grace. Show them that we are all one. Practice on earth what we will be doing in heaven. The greatest sound on earth is God's people declaring His holiness and might in one accord.

TWEET 17

#DEARWORSHIPLEADER WHAT YOU WEAR MATTERS. IF IT DON'T FIT, YOU MUST RELENT. PEOPLE ARE EASILY DISTRACTED.

Do not minimize the importance of what you wear when you are leading worship. Too many people overlook this area. When you stand in the front, you are asking people to look at you. And they will have to look at you for thirty minutes to an hour. It is distracting to worship God while looking at someone who is wearing something inappropriate, unclean, or that does not fit properly. The scripture says that men look on the outside but God looks at the heart. That scripture is true both ways. When you are worshipping God looks into your heart and sees your passion, love and desire to be closer to Him. The people you are singing in front of, though, cannot see that. They can only see your outside. And they are watching. Wear something that does not distract from the presence of God. The key is to know the dress code of the church. Understand what the culture of your church is and be in line with that.

TWEET 18

#DEARWORSHIPLEADER IF IT DOESN'T EXCITE YOU IT WON'T EXCITE THEM. LEARN TO LOVE THE SONG YOU'RE SINGING.

Tell me if you can relate- the song assignments for the month are sent and you are given a song to lead that you do not like. You try your best to wiggle out of it but nothing works. You try to trade songs with someone else, but they will not trade with you because they love their song. Every worship leader has a song or a style of music they do not like to sing. There are just some songs that do not match our voice or our style well. In those instances, the key is to change your perspective. Remind yourself that this is not a concert it is a worship experience. It is not about personal preference, but the sound of heaven needed in that moment and God's need of your personal submission to divine purpose. Embrace the song. The moment you embrace it is the moment you can express it with excitement and energy. Find the personal revelation in it and make the song your own. Then, turn it into the best song in that moment.

TWEET 19

#DEARWORSHIPLEADER IF THEY NEED MUSICAL TRAINING TO SING IT THEN IT'S PROBABLY TOO COMPLICATED. SIMPLE ALWAYS WINS.

As the worship leader, your main objective is to get the people to sing along with you. It is one of the things that differentiate a worship experience from a Broadway show. The people are not just spectators, but participators. They are not just the crowd they are the choir. Select songs they can sing. A song may seem rudimentary to you but to them it is just right. If a song is too complicated, the congregation will watch and stare in awe of your genius. When the song is one they can sing along to, they will worship the Lord and create their own altar at their seat. When you are worship leading, you are teaching songs that the congregation may not know but will learn under your tutelage. Use wisdom in choosing what to sing and how to sing it. Seek a way that is inviting and not intimidating.

TWEET 20

#DEARWORSHIPLEADER YOU MAY HAVE TO SING ANOTHER SONG. SO ALWAYS HAVE AN EXTRA ON HAND AND READY TO GO.

This has happened to me more times than I can count. You have created a four-song set that is incredible. You have rehearsed it for hours and everything is in place. You then execute the set to perfection and just when you think it is time to walk off the stage the production person gives you the signal to sing one more song. Your heart starts beating rapidly. Your palms get sweaty and your breathing becomes difficult. You do not have another song. At least not one that you rehearsed. Your mind starts pacing through your mental catalog of worship songs. Will this one work? Will the sopranos know this one? Can the musicians pick this up quickly? Here is my advice. Avoid all the stress of this situation by simply having an extra song prepared and in your reserve at all times. It will bring peace to you and to your Pastor.

TWEET 21

#DEARWORSHIPLEADER IF YOU KEEP TRYING TO "KILL THE ROOM" YOU WILL END UP KILLING YOUR VOICE. FLOW WITH THE SPIRIT AND LET THE SONG DICTATE THE DELIVERY.

Whenever a worship leader does a great job on a particular song, someone will come up to that leader and say, "You killed that song!" It is our way of saying you took all the life out of that song with your phenomenal singing. While this compliment encourages us, it can also make us go all out to try and "kill the room" every time. In hopes of getting those compliments, we may sing at a pitch and with a force that strains every vein in our throat. In our attempt to "kill that song", we end up killing our voice and destroying our vocal chords. The goal is not to out sing the song. The goal should be to find out what the song needs and flow within the moments within the song. A good song should feel like a story not a struggle. Leading a song is like taking people on a journey. You are their guide leading them to a particular destination. You do not want the ride to be bumpy; you want it to be smooth. If you really want the song to sound phenomenal then sing with it not over it. Find out what the song needs and give it that. Nothing more, nothing less.

TWEET 22

#DEARWORSHIPLEADER IF THE SONG IS NOT RIGHT, PUT IT TO FLIGHT. SAVE IT FOR ANOTHER DAY.

Growing up my mom would bake cakes all the time. It was a torturous process for me as a kid, because the house would be filled with this delightful aroma and I would be so ready to eat the cake that waiting felt like dying. Routinely, I would look through the steamed glass window into the oven and try to convince my mom the cake was done. She could now take it out so we could all eat it. My mother would say, "Son it looks done, but it still needs more time." Every time she said that I felt like she was lying. I mean clearly I was staring at a golden brown cake. But when she would open the oven and put a fork inside the cake, there would always be this uncooked batter stuck to the fork. Are you taking songs out the oven too soon? Are you presenting material to the congregation that has not been fully prepared all the way through? I know you love that song, but if it is not ready give it more time. It is better to wait and sing something that your team feels fully confident with. Let the song bake a little longer. If you "serve" the song after intense rehearsal and thorough practice, the congregation will taste and see that the Lord is good through powerful worship rather than become distracted with unnecessary blunders that could have been avoided with additional time.

TWEET 23

#DEARWORSHIPLEADER IT'S GOING TO SOUND STRANGE IF IT'S NOT IN YOUR RANGE. LET SOMEONE ELSE SING IT.

My mentor always laughs at me when we play basketball. He laughs because whenever I get on the court the first few shots I take are way out behind the three-point line. He always screams at me to move in closer. "Brian, why do you always try and shoot so far from the basket? Why not move in closer for an easier shot?" I like to take the three pointers because it is more difficult. It is more challenging. Going for a layup would be easy, but who wants to do the easy thing? The problem with my method is that I always miss. Shot after shot I miss again and again. The issue is that I am shooting out of my range. If I would just move in a little bit closer to the basket, I would make more shots. The same is true with singing. The goal is to sing in your range. When you are in your range, you are winning. You give out the sweetest and purest sound possible. It is pleasant to listen to and easy on your voice. When you start trying to shoot vocal three pointers that are out of your range, you produce a sound that pierces the ears and causes damage to your vocal chords. If you have to grab your ear, twist your head, and step onto your tiptoes to hit that note then it is probably out of your range. If your veins look like they are getting ready to break through your neck when you are singing, then it is more likely than not that you are out of your range. I know how it feels to want to take the song higher and higher and higher, but if you keep your feet on the ground, you will score so many more points by simply staying in your range.

TWEET 24

#DEARWORSHIPLEADER THE ANOINTING WILL COST YOU SOMETHING. SOMETIMES THE SACRIFICE OF PRAISE WILL COST YOU THE SACRIFICE OF PLEASURE.

Everyone wants the stage but very few want to go through the stages. If you want to go beyond talent and into the anointing you will have to sacrifice something. God will often challenge you to let go of something you want, or think you need, in order to pull you deeper into fellowship with Him. Giving up things that we want can be painful but it pales in comparison to all the benefits we receive from Christ. Do not just be gifted be anointed. Break away from the hindrances and habits that take you away from His glory. The more you are willing to give up for Him the more of Him you will get.

TWEET 25

#DEARWORSHIPLEADER THERE IS A DIFFERENCE BETWEEN SINGING THE SONG AND RELEASING THE SOUND. YOU MUST DO BOTH.

You can rehearse the songs, but you can only hear the sound. There are moments in a worship set where something just flows from within your spirit and becomes a prophetic chant piercing the atmosphere in the room. It is not something you practiced or anything you have sung before. Sometimes it is a sentence, a word, or even a moan. It is spontaneous and supernatural. Whether your worship time is an hour or only fifteen minutes you must listen for the melody that the Lord puts into your heart while you are singing. A good song will move you but a prophetic sound will transform you. Sing each song with your ears open for God to pour something new and fresh into your spirit.

TWEET 26

#DEARWORSHIPLEADER IT IS GOING TO BE DIFFICULT TO DO IN PUBLIC WHAT YOU HAVE NEVER DONE IN PRIVATE. DON'T JUST BE A WORSHIP LEADER BE A WORSHIPPER.

You cannot lead me somewhere you have never been. You cannot guide me to a place you have not seen. I cannot follow you if you do not know where you are going. A worship leader must first be a worshipper. The more time you spend in God's presence alone the better you will be at leading others into it corporately. Worship is not a routine; it is a way of living. It is a way of being. It is an attitude of the heart, soul, and mind. To lead worship effectively you have to be able to hear from God. You have to be able to follow His leading and be in sync with the Spirit. You cannot follow a voice you have never heard. Plan time alone with God. Hear His voice. Feel His presence. Cry before Him with tears of repentance and honor. Learn the names of God and worship Him around every name. Be a worshipper at your core and your leading will go to another level.

TWEET 27

#DEARWORSHIPLEADER IF YOU CAN STAND FOR THE SINGING YOU CAN SIT FOR THE SERMON. YOU NEED A WORD TOO.

As worship leaders, we have a tendency to "tap out" once we are done with our part. We exert so much energy on the stage that once we are done we are ready to leave, grab something to eat and go home. Leading worship and then leaving the service sends the wrong message to your church, the pastor, and to yourself. Worship is only one part of the service. The preached word is another part of the service. As much as the pastor needs your worship, you need to hear their word. Their teaching will ground you and replenish all that you poured out during worship. If you can lead worship, you can receive the word. I know that you are tired. I know you got to the church before everybody else. I know you have been standing longer than anyone else in the building has. Rather than hang out in the back or just leave, it will benefit you greatly to sit and soak in the sermon. You will be blessed by it.

(The only exception to this rule is worship leaders who lead at churches that have multiple services. In that case, you can stay for one or stay for all based on the desire of the senior pastor. Do not make assumptions. Find out from the Senior Pastor what they prefer first. More often than not, they will want you to be a part of at least one full service.)

TWEET 28

#DEARWORSHIPLEADER GOD LOVES YOU. LET THAT BE ENOUGH.

Beyond the applause, compliments, and accolades, let the fact that God loves you be the driving force of who you are. God loves you so much that He sent His one and only Son to die for you on a cross. He took your punishment. He paid your ransom. He sacrificed His life so that you could be free from the bondage of sin, the chains of guilt and shame, and the penalty of eternal separation from God. If God would give up Jesus for you, what would He possibly withhold from you? God loves you with an unconditional love. The love of people, however, is based on conditions. They love you as long as you are doing what they want you to do or saying what they want you to say. God loved you when you were a sinner. He stuck by you when you were His enemy. God loves you beyond words and at some point that has to be enough for you. If they never call your name, cheer your accomplishments, or appreciate all you have done- it is ok. There is One who knows all things and He will reward you just because you are His own.

TWEET 29

#DEARWORSHIPLEADER IF YOU CAN'T MOVE GOD THEN YOU CAN'T MOVE THE PEOPLE. SING TO IMPRESS HIM NOT THEM.

Even though we stand before an audience of many we are only singing for an audience of One. Our aim is to please God. We want to cultivate an environment that causes Heaven to fill our earth. If Heaven is not pleased, then our singing has no meaning. Worship is not about what you do, it is about Who we do it for. We sing and dance because of the King of kings. We shout and celebrate because Jesus has won the victory. We are singing for Him, about Him, and to Him. If He is not drawn to your worship, then no one else will be. Mentally prepare yourself to engage Christ with your worship. He said, "If you will draw nigh unto me, I will draw nigh unto you." If you draw Him, He will come in close. And when He comes in close, He will consume every heart and fill every soul. Do not worry about impressing people with your talent. Focus on attracting Heaven with your brokenness. Sing for Him not for them.

TWEET 30

#DEARWORSHIPLEADER NEVER GET SO CAUGHT UP WITH THE TITLE THAT YOU LOSE SIGHT OF THE THRONE. IT'S HIS KINGDOM, NOT YOURS.

People love titles. They make us feel important. They give us a sense of accomplishment and success. Everybody wants a title but few people want the weight of responsibility that comes with it. Being a worship leader is a privilege. It is an honor to bear that position in life. However, it is easy to be so caught up with the title that you forget what the assignment is really about. You can get addicted to the attention, the compliments, and the perks of holding the title that you lose your hunger and desperation for God. Never get attached to the title. Stay in pursuit of His throne. Keep the Lord at the forefront of all that you do. Titles come and go but your relationship with God will remain forever. Positions come and go. But your position in Christ is secure. Never let your position in life outweigh your position in Christ. Be more confident in the fact that you are positioned in His love, anchored in His grace and grounded in His power. If you really want to brag about your title then brag about these titles- favored, cherished, anointed, loved, forgiven, blessed. Post these titles on your social media pages. Put them on your business cards. Rejoice over these titles and not the title of worship leader. Never let people put a crown on your head that makes you feel like you are the king of the stage. We are not building your kingdom. We are not advancing your career. We are not adding to your portfolio. We are building the Kingdom for the advancement of the church. Stay focused on what matters.

TWEET 31

#DEARWORSHIPLEADER THE CROWD MAY NOT RESPOND THE WAY YOU WANT THEM TO. WORSHIP ANYWAY.

Never be distracted by the response of the crowd. Do not let the level of their reaction dictate the level of your worship. Some worship leaders are prisoners to crowd response. If the congregation looks like they are into it, then we feel good. If it looks like they are not, then we feel horrible. However, this is not a concert. We are there to create an atmosphere where an encounter with Christ can happen. We are there to model what worship looks like and lead them to sing with us. It is not about their excitement, it is about ours. The fire that comes in worship has to come from the inside of you not from the outside. You have to come with your own passion. You must have the ability to stir yourself up and create your own energy. If you need the people shouting in order for you to worship effectively, then something is wrong. Let the fire begin in you. Let the worship experience start in your core and be poured out to the Lord on behalf of others. If no one sings along, keep worshipping. If no one gives a big standing ovation, just worship anyway. If no one sheds a tear, worship anyway. The Lord is listening and He inhabits your praise. He enjoys your singing and your worship. Sing for an audience of one. Do not let God behold you watching the people, let the people watch you beholding God.

#DEARWORSHIPLEADER IF YOU CAN'T FALL AT HIS FEET YOU CAN'T RECEIVE FROM HIS HAND.

The truth of the matter is that God wants to bless you. He wants to bless you beyond your wildest imagination. He is a generous God. There is nothing stingy about Him. He will bless your home, your health, your family, your career, and anything else you bring before Him. It is not a struggle for Him to bless you. He is full of resources. Heaven is not experiencing a recession and it is not going through a drought. Heaven is full of what you need for when you need it. But just because God wants to bless you does not mean He wants to be your personal genie. God is not the lottery. You cannot play the right numbers or scratch the right boxes in order to get your prize. He is the Creator and we are the creation. He is the Potter and we are the clay. He is the shepherd and we are the sheep. Worship is when we bow down our agenda, our identity, and our weaknesses at the feet of Jesus. It is the place where we acknowledge His lordship over our lives. If you only want His blessings and not His lordship then you will never experience the beauty of relationship with the Father. Do not just seek the blessings from His hand; seek the bowing at His feet. For it is there that you will discover brokenness and closeness with God. To be close to Him is the greatest blessing of all.

TWEET 33

#DEARWORSHIPLEADER IF YOU ABUSE THE POSITION YOU WILL LOSE THE PLATFORM. KEEP YOURSELF IN CHECK.

As a worship leader, you have great influence in the lives of people. Not only do they look to you as a worship leader, they also look to you as a leader in the church and in the community. What you say carries weight. How you behave and conduct yourself impacts others. Be mindful of the power you hold. If you use that power to add value to others and be a great representation of Christ, you will increase in influence and wisdom. But if you abuse that power to advance your personal agenda and create divisiveness in the church then eventually you will lose that power and the platform. Be mindful how you treat people. Pay attention to what you say about the pastor and the church. Avoid cliques and gossip. Because of the amount of compliments we get, the amount of time we are on stage, and the weightiness of our gift, we can start to think that we are more powerful than the pastor is. We can create mini movements in the church centered around us. Run from the temptation to be lifted above your assignment. Let love lead you. Let peace guide you. Be nice. Walk in humility. Stay low and use your influence to change a generation.

TWEET 34

#DEARWORSHIPLEADER ALWAYS POINT THE ATTENTION BACK TO HIM. YOU'RE A GUIDE NOT A GOD. MAKE SURE THAT'S EXTREMELY CLEAR.

I will never forget the day when my Bishop at the time walked on stage after a worship set and made an announcement to the church. He said that we would no longer be singing horizontal songs during worship, only vertical. At the time, I had no idea what he was referring to. I had never heard the terms horizontal songs and vertical songs. To me they were all just regular songs. Then he explained that horizontal songs are songs we sing to each other and they are about us. But vertical songs are songs that we sing to the Lord and they are all about Him. Worship is vertical not horizontal. From that day, we only sang songs that were to God and about God. It revolutionized our church and our culture. This is a picture of what the spirit of the worship leader is all about. We are constantly deflecting the attention off us and onto Him. We may hold the mic but he holds the might. Let His name constantly reign over yours. It is ok to say thank you when people honor you for your faithfulness and commitment. Yet, be commended for your ability to be a guide, not a god. You are an arrow that is aimed towards Heaven. You are the finger that is pointing to Jesus. You are but a branch, while He is the vine. Apart from Him you can do nothing. Never allow people or their accolades detach you from the Source and reason for what you do.

TWEET 35

#DEARWORSHIPLEADER DON'T REBUKE THE DEVIL MORE THAN YOU REVERENCE GOD. SATAN IS UNDER YOUR FEET. THE SAVIOR IS ABOVE YOUR HEAD. LOOK UP.

Imagine sitting down with your spouse to enjoy a nice dinner at a fancy restaurant. The table is filled with candles and the view is absolutely stunning. As you grab their hand and look into their eyes, you lean in and ask them about their day and what is on their mind. In response to your question, they proceed to tell you about their ex. For the next thirty minutes they go into a long diatribe about how they cannot stand their ex, how dumb they are, and how they hope they never see them again. Imagine how devastated you would feel. Think about the message that they are sending to you. Here you are loyal, faithful, loving, and generous, and all they want to talk about is the person they hate. That is what it looks like when we spend thirty minutes of rebuking the devil during worship and three minutes thanking God for what He has done. The Bible says, "Let God arise and let His enemies be scattered." If you lift the name of Jesus, the enemy will have no room to take over your service. I know you want to bind him and rebuke him, curse him and cast him out. However, do not let that be the driving force of your worship. Do not give the enemy more attention than you give God. If you resist the devil, he will flee.

TWEET 36

#DEARWORSHIPLEADER NEVER MISTAKE THEIR APPLAUSE FOR HIM AS APPLAUSE FOR YOU. STAY IN YOUR LANE.

There is the story of a father who went fishing with his son. For hours, they were out in the middle of the river talking and waiting to catch some fish. The son was becoming irritated at his inability to catch any fish. He was getting bored and was ready to call it quits. Of course his father was catching all kinds of fish. He was great at it and knew what he was doing. While the son was not looking his father took one of the fish and put it on the end of the boy's hook. Then he quickly threw the hook back into the water. The father excitedly encouraged his son to check the hook again to see if he had caught anything. Discouraged, the son half-heartedly pulled his hook out of the water. To the boy's surprise, there was a fish at the end of his hook. He was filled with so much excitement and accomplishment. The moment they arrived home, the son burst through the doors screaming at the top of his lungs, "Look what I did! Look what I caught! Look at my fish!" The son had no idea that he really had not caught anything, but that his father had provided it for him. We are like the son in the story. Our gifts and anointing may make us feel like we have accomplished something great. We must never mistake what we do for what God did. It is His anointing. It is His gift. It is His power that enables us to do what we do. Before we run through the church yelling for everyone to look at what we did, we must be sure to give proper credit to who it is due. If the power of God is present as you worship, it is not your singing that amazes people, it is His presence filling them. If the anointing falls and the spirit of

God moves during a service, it is not your vocal runs or new dance routine that is making the impact. It is the glory of God hovering over the room. Never take credit for what God does. Give the glory to God and He will continue to move in the atmospheres you worship.

TWEET 37

#DEARWORSHIPLEADER IF YOU ONLY GIVE A PRAISE OFFERING AND NEVER A FINANCIAL OFFERING YOU ARE ROBBING YOURSELF OF MAJOR BLESSINGS.

Unfortunately, worship leaders are not always the best financial givers. In fact, oftentimes we are in the pulpit with a microphone in our hands when the time of giving takes place. Many people think that worship is that thing you do before the offering starts and right after the offering is over. The truth is, though, the offering is still a part of worship. If you can give God your ministry but not your money, you are skipping out on part of the worship experience. When you join in with the congregation to give of your finances you create a greater bond between the pulpit and the pew. It is a sign of agreement. It is a sign of maturity.

TWEET 38

#DEARWORSHIPLEADER YOU SEND THE WRONG MESSAGE WHEN YOU GIVE A CHURCH YOUR TALENT BUT NOT YOUR TITHE. THERE CANNOT BE TRUE WORSHIP WITHOUT TRUE SACRIFICE.

Confession: I was not always a faithful tither when I began leading worship. I was inconsistent and nonchalant with my giving. A part of me felt like I was already giving so much of my time and talent to the church that no one would really miss my tithe. I soon realized, however, that I loved worship leading so much that giving my talent and my time were not really major sacrifices for me. Giving my money was. Worship at its core is a sacrifice. You will experience your greatest level of worship at your greatest level of sacrifice. When I began tithing consistently, I was amazed at how much it affected my worship leading. I was finally in full agreement with my church and was able to experience the spiritual power that comes with being in agreement. Giving your tithe to your church is not just an obligation it's an incredible opportunity to trust God at a deeper level.

TWEET 39

#DEARWORSHIPLEADER IF YOU CAN'T HONOR THE CHURCH YOU DON'T DESERVE AN HONORARIUM.

It is your highest priority to honor the church where you lead worship. Honor them with your words, your presence, your agreement, and your prayers. You cannot separate *what you do* for the church from *what you say* about the church. No church is perfect. No church has it all together. Yet, it does not stand a chance of getting better if you keep cursing it with your words. It is hypocritical to collect a check from a church you dishonor. If the church is so bad, why would you want to take their money? Clearly, you have found something good about it. Never, ever, ever, ever, dishonor and disrespect the church that has invested financial resources into you. It is possible to fool people, but you cannot fool God. If you can speak blessings and not cursing, if you can take your feelings to your prayer room, if you can hold your peace and let the Lord fight your battles, you will see bountiful blessings in your life.

TWEET 40

#DEARWORSHIPLEADER THEY MAY FORGET YOUR CHECK. FORGIVE THEM. AND BRING THE FIRE ANYWAY.

It can be very frustrating when a church tells you they will compensate you and then, right before the service starts or, even worse, after the service ends, they tell you that they forgot the check. Your heart breaks. You feel like you were lied to, as if someone took advantage of you. It can create a resentful feeling in your heart and make you bitter toward that church. As tough as it is, you have to forgive them and worship with fire in your heart anyway. You have to trust that God will reward your faithfulness and that He knows what you need. You do not have to retaliate by giving a half-hearted effort during worship. You do not need to go on social media and blast the church. You must do what you have been called to do. Never let a bad situation interfere with your ability to lead worship. You have to lead when you are feeling good and you have to lead when you are feeling horrible. *Being a worship leader is not about your feelings, it is about your assignment.* Be faithful to your assignment and God will open doors that you cannot imagine.

TWEET 41

#DEARWORSHIPLEADER THE CONGREGATION CAN FALL OUT BUT YOU CAN'T. YOU CANNOT LEAD THEM IF YOU LEAVE THEM STARING AT AN EMPTY STAGE.

As a worship leader, it is great to be energetic, expressive, and even emotional. Just do not be out of control. Do not get so lost in your worshipping that you forget about the congregation, the singers, and the band. *That is not worship leading that is worship leaving.* You are on stage for a reason. You are in the front for a reason. Everything you do is to be a model for the people watching you. If you leave them without direction and instruction so that you can fall out on the side of the stage and have your own personal time with the Lord then you have created confusion. I hear people say, "Well, we have to let the Lord have His way." That is not the *Lord* having *His* way, that is **YOU** having **YOUR** way. You are trying to have a moment with God in public that you should have had in private. It is not about you. It is about everyone.

TWEET 42

#DEARWORSHIPLEADER DO NOT YELL AT THE CONGREGATION. YOU ARE NOT THEIR SHEPHERD.

Be a worship leader, not a drill sergeant. I know it is frustrating when you are worshipping with all of your heart and soul only to look out into the crowd and see a group of people who look like they have been frozen in time. It can be deflating when the congregation is not participating with the energy you would like to see. However, you cannot command them into participating. I have seen worship leaders yell, scream, make angry faces, and demean people from the stage. That is not the solution. Your assignment is to create an atmosphere so welcoming that anyone can join in when they are ready. You are to model for them what worship looks like. Jesus said, "If I be lifted up I will draw all men unto me." Your responsibility is to lift Him up. His responsibility is to draw all men. *Be the lifter, not the drawer.* Leave that to Jesus and the pastor. You just do the lifting. Be so good at lifting the name of Jesus that people do not even notice you. When they are captivated by Jesus, they will worship on their own.

TWEET 43

#DEARWORSHIPLEADER IF YOU SHOW THEM THEY'LL FOLLOW. IF YOU SHOUT AT THEM THEY'LL FALTER. BE THE MODEL NOT THE MONSTER.

When you stand before a congregation, never assume that everyone knows what to do when worship begins. So often we erroneously assume everyone knows why we lift our hands, clap, sing, or dance before the Lord. The truth is many people in the audience spend weeks observing you before they join in. People need to feel comfortable in an environment before they can feel free to let down their guard. Be patient. Love. Possess a gentle spirit. There are so many factors that prevent people from worshipping. Sometimes it is outside stress. Then there are times when the distractions are within the church. It is possible they are nervous, shy, or just do not like to sing. Whatever the case may be prayerfully, seek God on how to create an environment that produces unrestrained worshippers.

TWEET 44

#DEARWORSHIPLEADER JUST BECAUSE YOU ARE ANOINTED DOESN'T MEAN YOU'RE ADMINISTRATIVE. FIND A VOLUNTEER WHO CAN HELP YOU.

You do not have to do this on your own. Whether you are paid staff or unpaid staff, you should try to identify someone administrative who can help you. Just because you can sing, play an instrument, and move a room with worship does not mean you are good with emails, phone calls, and data entry. Solicit the help of faithful volunteers who are gifted in administration. Even if you have incredible administrative gifts, it would still be wise to delegate some of these responsibilities. It is great to be anointed. However, when you can add strong administration to a ministry that is highly anointed you have super power. God loves order and He blesses structure. Increase your productivity and effectiveness by creating an administrative team to help you.

TWEET 45

#DEARWORSHIPLEADER THEY NEED YOUR SET LIST WELL IN ADVANCE. YOU AND GOD CAN'T BE THE ONLY ONES WITH THE SONGS.

If you are anything like me, you want to be inspired when you pick your set of worship songs. You want God to give you the right songs for that specific day. You are hoping to select the ultimate worship set of songs that will have everyone on their feet worshipping from the first song to the last. Picking songs this way takes concentration, it takes focus, it takes isolation from everyone around you, and unfortunately, it takes forever. There are so many people who need your set list. And they need it early. Production needs your set list to do their lights and lyrics. The band needs your song list so they can prepare the music for rehearsal. The background vocalists need your set list so they can learn the lyrics and melodies on their own. You need to have your song list ready at the beginning of the month for the entire month. The same God who can speak to you at the last minute can also speak to you well in advance. You will love the freedom that comes with being prepared early and your team will appreciate you for helping them do their jobs better.

TWEET 46

#DEARWORSHIPLEADER THE SOUND ENGINEER IS YOUR FRIEND. TREAT THEM WELL AND THEY WILL HELP YOU. TREAT THEM WRONG AND THEY WILL MESS WITH YOUR MICROPHONE.

It is critical that you have a great relationship with the sound engineer. Greet them. Celebrate them privately and publicly. Show appreciation for their work. Bring them some coffee and donuts. Do whatever you need to do to build a positive rapport with them. If you do, you will be astonished at the treatment you will receive. They will pay attention to detail. They will give you that nice reverb at just the right moment. They will fill your ears with the sweetest sounds coming from the monitor. And when things go wrong they will go out of their way to try to fix it for you. However, if you ignore them, berate them, or talk to them like they are unskilled children, they will feel deflated around you. When there is feedback coming from your monitor, they will be slow to fix it. When you need more volume, they will pretend they do not notice. Treat your sound engineer well. You need them. They help you create a sound that leads people before God. Bless them and they will bless you.

TWEET 47

#DEARWORSHIPLEADER BE NICE TO THE BAND. YOU ARE GOING TO NEED THEM TO COVER YOU AT SOME POINT.

The relationship between the worship leader and the band is critical. It is like peanut butter and jelly...cereal and milk...rice and beans...grits and sugar... (Ok maybe not that last one... but you get the picture). When the worship team and the band are in sync, it is incredible. There is a supernatural sound and an effortless flow that creates a glorious atmosphere of worship. In the same way, when the relationship is not good it creates tension and friction within the presentation. Heaven cannot flow through disagreement. The power is in coming together- with *one* mind, *one* heart and *one* mission. That single purpose is to lead people into the presence of God. If there is tension between you and the band, pray for reconciliation. Make every effort to create a cohesive environment. Connect outside of church. Do not take the "I'm just going to do my job and leave" attitude. It does not work. If you will show peace to the band, they will show peace to you. And they will play for you like they have never played for you before.

TWEET 48

#DEARWORSHIPLEADER IF YOU DON'T CORRECT IT, IT'LL GET OUT OF CONTROL. IF YOU DON'T CONFRONT IT, IT WON'T CHANGE. YOUR TEAM IS LONGING FOR YOUR LEADERSHIP.

The toughest part of being a worship leader is instilling in others the same zeal and passion that you carry. Singing before the Lord is natural. However, it takes work to create a culture, vision, and team that reflects your heart. You are not the worship leader just because you can sing. You are the leader because you can organize a team and build a culture of worship that will influence the entire church. Your team does not need your singing they need your leading. Build them. Pour into them. Teach them not only what to do but why it is being done. If something is out of control, you have to deal with it. You set the tone. They are waiting for your instruction. They want you to set the vision and make it so plain that they can run with it. You are not there just to teach songs, you are there to teach sacrifice. You are there to show them what it looks like to sacrifice your time and talent for God, the church, and each other. Do not just lead on the stage, lead in the choir room. If you lead them, they will not only follow, but also reproduce what has been instilled in them.

TWEET 49

#DEARWORSHIPLEADER EVERY NOW AND THEN DO SOMETHING FUN WITH YOUR VOLUNTEERS. LET THEM SEE THAT YOU'RE NOT A SUPERHERO ALL THE TIME!

Most of the time when our volunteers see us we are in work mode. We are working with the band, running a rehearsal, teaching voices, or planning the next set. Rarely do they see us outside of church. Very few ever see us laughing or enjoying ourselves outside of the four walls. Every now and then, plan an outing with your team. Take them bowling or do a spontaneous potluck dinner at a volunteer's house. I recognize the need to be separate from your team. If the relationship is too friendly it can be difficult to challenge, correct, or confront them later on. It is ok to be separate sometimes, but it is not ok to be separate all the time. You are asking a lot from your volunteers. You are hoping that they will make sacrifices for the team that may even rival their families and full time jobs. To do so consistently, there must be a relationship. It is difficult to ask for someone's hand when you have completely ignored their heart. Spend some personal time with your volunteers. Learn their name and their stories. It will help you have more grace for their challenges and a better perspective to pray from. Take off your cape. Step out of the phone booth. Let them see your Clark Kent for a little while.

TWEET 50

#DEARWORSHIPLEADER DEFEND YOUR TEAM AND THEY'LL DEFEND YOU. EXPOSE THEM AND THEY'LL EXPOSE YOU.

A good worship leader wants to see their team succeed. The more successful your team, the more successful you are as the leader. These are people who give of their time to sing with you, pray for you, and stand behind you week after week. They arrive at the church just as early as you do. They attend the same amount of rehearsals as you do. They stand for the same amount of hours as you. They do all of this without getting any credit or recognition for their work. Your team may not be perfect, but they are yours. Treat them well. Do not throw them under the bus when they falter. Do not be quick to put them on blast for every error. They cover your mistakes all the time. If you defend them in public, you will earn their trust. When they see you standing up for them they will take a stand for you. Take care of your team and I promise they will take care of you.

TWEET 51

#DEARWORSHIPLEADER YOUR TEAM WILL LISTEN TO WHAT YOU SAY BUT THEY WILL IMITATE WHAT YOU DO. NEVER DEMAND WHAT YOU DO NOT DEMONSTRATE.

Your team will be a reflection of the real you. Not the version that gives great speeches and sings great songs. They will reflect what you do not what you say. No matter how many speeches you give about unity within the team, if you are divisive, they will be too. No matter how many times you demand that the team show up on time, if you are late, they will be too. You can give the greatest presentation on the need for more prayer in their personal lives, but if you do not pray, they will not either. No matter which way you look at it, your team is a mirror of the real you. If there is gossip in your team, it is because you gossip. If people talk about the church in a disrespectful manner, it is because they have heard you do it. You cannot ask your team to be what you are not. The only way they can do that is if they get a new leader. This should encourage you, though. Because it means if you pray more, give more, work more, forgive more, and worship, more your team will follow your example.

TWEET 52

#DEARWORSHIPLEADER DON'T CUFF THE MIC. THE SOUND ENGINEER HATES IT AND WE DON'T HEAR YOU THAT CLEARLY.

I am guilty of this one. Lock me up and throw away the key. I am famous for cuffing the microphone. I do not know why I do it. There is just something cool about it. For me it creates a sound that I like. Unfortunately, it makes it difficult for people to hear you and for the sound engineer to control your microphone. I have been on stage countless times with my full hand cuffed around the top of the microphone only to look up and see the sound engineer giving me crazy signals to stop. Of course, I try my best to stop, but at some point without me being conscious of it, I cuff it again. I have learned to stop. Let me rephrase. I have learned to do it less. The preacher in me likes to cuff the microphone. However, I recognize that it is not always pleasant to the ears. I want the people to hear me clearly. I want the sound engineer to like working with me. I do not want to complicate their job. So I had to put this tweet out there to save some other worship leader from being yelled at in the future as many times as I have in the past.

TWEET 53

#DEARWORSHIPLEADER IF YOU DON'T USE YOUR MONITOR YOU WILL LOSE YOUR MIND AND YOUR VOICE. DO A SOUND CHECK.

I have worked out with many fitness trainers in my life. Not that I am a workout warrior or anything, but I find myself needing the occasional push from a trainer. When I work out with a trainer they always make me stretch prior to the workout. Now, I have a personal problem with stretching. For me, it is boring. I want to get to the fun stuff. Let's lift some weights. Give me the dumbbells. Make me do some pushups. Instead they make me stretch for fifteen minutes. I always think to myself, "Are they doing this just to pass the time? Is this portion of the workout really necessary?" Well if you have ever felt the cramps that come in your leg when you do not stretch, you know that the time is very necessary. No matter how you feel about doing sound checks, they must be done. A good sound check will prevent you from straining your voice because you cannot hear yourself. A sound check will ensure that everybody gets to hear exactly what they need so that they can sing at their best. If you skip the sound check you will be forced to spend the first twenty minutes of your worship set staring at the sound engineer, giving him hand signals as if you are directing a fleet of planes on a tarmac. That is not fair to the audience or to your team. Moreover, it will eventually wear on your voice. Train your team to take sound checks seriously. Create a culture that arrives early so you can get the right levels. It will enhance the quality of your sound and protect the gift that God gave you.

TWEET 54

#DEARWORSHIPLEADER END REHEARSAL ON TIME. YOUR TEAM WILL THANK YOU.

Time is important. It is more important today than it has ever been before. People are balancing families, careers, and recreational activities. They are trying to find time to sleep, study, workout, and play with their children. One of the best ways to honor a person is by honoring their time. When you honor a person's time you communicate to them that you value their sacrifice and appreciate their commitment. You must value the time of your volunteers. Many of them come to rehearsal straight from work. Some have to find babysitters for their children. Regardless of the circumstance, it is vital that you show them the importance of time. Many worship leaders complain that their team does not show up on time. There are many reasons that people show up late. I have found, though, that people do not come on time because rehearsal does not end on time. Since they know they will be there later than scheduled, they tend to show up later than they are supposed to. If rehearsal ends at noon, end at noon. If it ends at eight in the evening, end at eight. Create a culture of structure, excellence, and consistency.

TWEET 55

#DEARWORSHIPLEADER IF YOU DON'T KNOW THE LYRICS NEITHER WILL YOUR TEAM. THEY ARE A REFLECTION OF YOUR WORK HABITS.

"Practice. We are talking about practice. Practice. Not the game. Not the game. We are in here talking about practice." This was the infamous speech given by NBA superstar Allen Iverson. He made this statement during a press conference where he was being questioned about his practice habits. His coach had come out and complained to the press that his star player did not like to practice and that it was having a negative effect on the rest of the team. Sometimes when you are very talented and gifted in a particular area you can form bad work habits because things that are difficult for others come easier to you. I have been guilty of this as a worship leader. I have fumbled a time or two, or three or four, on knowing all the lyrics to the songs. Thank God for screens and a great multimedia department. Because I have been leading worship for most of my life, I, too, can start to get too comfortable with my surroundings and rely on my talent rather than my work ethic. What I realized is if I am doing this, then so are the people around me. They take their cues from me. If I am not prepared when I come to rehearsal neither will they. It is critical that I know the song, the lyrics and the direction I want it to go. Now with that being said we are by no means legalistic when it comes to this. Everyone makes mistakes. And sometimes the occasional slip up leads to a lot of laughter and joking. The key is to communicate hard work and preparation to your team. Make it part of the culture and you will reproduce it in others even when you are not around.

TWEET 56

#DEARWORSHIPLEADER YOU MUST LEARN THE ART OF SINGING AND SIGNALING. DON'T LEAD THE CROWD AND LOSE THE BAND.

I have never had to direct traffic, but I can imagine it is a difficult job. What a juggling act it must be trying to direct one lane of traffic while staying alert to the other lane, all while watching out for the people who may be crossing in the crosswalk. In the same way, worship leaders direct a lot of traffic. We have to ensure that everyone is headed in the right direction. We have to cue the singers, while simultaneously signaling the band. If you are going to take your worship leading to the next level, you have to master the art of signaling. Everyone is watching you. They are not only getting their energy from you, but they are also getting their instructions from you. The band wants to know how many times you are going to repeat the chorus. They are looking to you to tell them when to cut out certain instruments, when to end the song, whether to reprise it or not. You hold all the answers. Singing is not enough. You must be able to lead everyone. Signaling does not mean yelling in the microphone giving instructions. It is about hand signals, body gestures, facial expressions, and subtle movements. You should have so much chemistry with your team and musicians that they know where you are going without you having to say a word. Teach them your rhythms and let them into your personality so that each week feels like a journey.

TWEET 57

#DEARWORSHIPLEADER YOU MUST KNOW A HYMN. YES, THEY ARE OLD. BUT, THEY'RE STILL GOLD. ALWAYS HAVE ONE READY.

I love the new contemporary worship songs. They are anointed, dynamic, and easy to sing. There is still something about church hymns that carry a powerful weight to them. Hymns may not have the cool chord progressions or catchy lyrics that our contemporary songs possess, but they are full of life giving power and doctrinal truth. While we may not be able to sing them for an entire worship set, we can certainly sprinkle them in from time to time. Hymns are part of our tradition. They are songs that were birthed in struggle and hardship. They are songs that were written by people who suffered for the gospel and triumphed over many trials. In our love for the new, let's not kill the old. Whether you attend a traditional church or a contemporary church, a large congregation or a small one, a church full of the Baby Boomers or Millennials, hymns will expand the depth of your worship experience.

TWEET 58

#DEARWORSHIPLEADER LEARN HOW TO SING WITH FLASHING LIGHTS AND FOG MACHINES. THEY AREN'T GOING ANYWHERE. SO EMBRACE IT.

At some point in your worship leading experience, you will have to sing with bright lights beaming in your face and throat closing haze machines flowing all around you. For some worship leaders this is the setting you have always dreamed of. For others this is a singing nightmare that disrupts your ability to lead effectively. Some worship leaders like to see the crowd. They feed off the interaction with the people. For others, the lights and fog can create physical difficulty, making the stage hotter or drier. As uncomfortable as it may be, you must get used to singing in **ANY** setting. As a leader, you must be able to function in a broad range of circumstances. Strong leaders must not be rattled by anything happening around them. Lights, fog machines, and cameras are there to enhance the worship experience for the audience. It creates a particular mood that is necessary for the majority of worshipers. The key is to focus on worship. Let the production team manage all the other things happening on the stage. Be prepared. Know your set completely. Drink plenty of water and embrace the environment you are in.

TWEET 59

#DEARWORSHIPLEADER YOU MUST BE ABLE TO LEAD WORSHIP IN DIFFERENT STYLES OF MUSIC. IF YOU CAN ONLY SING IN ONE GENRE, YOU WILL ONLY REACH ONE GROUP.

The church of Jesus Christ is the most dynamic and diverse movement in the world. The gospel of Jesus is being proclaimed in every nation, among every ethnicity, and in every language. People say that music is a universal language. In addition to that, worship is a universal language. There are few things more beautiful than watching people from different cultures sing together before the Lord. As a worship leader, you want to be able to sing and minister to people outside of your own culture. Do not be boxed in by your denomination, race, or ethnicity. The kingdom is so much bigger than that. The same Holy Spirit that fills your church also fills churches in Asia, Africa, Europe, and all through the continents of the world. Fellowship with worship leaders outside of your immediate circle. Expand your musical genre so that you can lead people from different backgrounds to the one true King. When we get to Heaven we will all be singing with one accord. We will be one body and one family under God. Let's practice on earth what we will experience in Heaven. Tear down the walls of religion; build relationships, and connections with all believers.

TWEET 60

#DEARWORSHIPLEADER IF YOU CAN'T STAND THE PASTOR PLEASE DON'T STAND IN THEIR PULPIT. THERE'S JUST TOO MUCH POLLUTION IN THAT PRAISE.

Nothing destroys a worship team's success more than a worship leader who does not like the Senior Pastor. It does not matter how talented you are, how well you can lead, or how great your singing is, if you do not like the Pastor then you should not stand in their pulpit. It is disloyal and dishonorable. Regardless of how you feel about the Pastor, it is because of them that you are on that stage. They are allowing you the opportunity to serve in your gift. They are sharing their platform and influence with you. If you do not like them, tell them. If it cannot be resolved then you should resign. Allow someone else with the willingness and capacity to honor their Pastor to grow with them in that position. Do not hold it hostage and spew pollution throughout the church. It is better that you resign and find a Pastor you like than to stay and make everyone miserable. Also, know that your team is watching you. As much as you think you are hiding how you feel, you are transferring your poison on to them. People will do what you say, but they will become who you are. Trust God and find where you belong.

TWEET 61

#DEARWORSHIPLEADER SING MORE, TALK LESS. THERE IS A SERMON COMING AFTER YOU.

Have you ever ordered so many appetizers at a restaurant that by the time the main course came you were too full to eat? That has happened to me countless times. Somehow, a T-bone steak just does not taste the same when you are full of mozzarella sticks and chicken kabobs. Now, rather than filling your hunger, you feel overwhelmed and stuffed. I have had to discipline myself to go with the salad before a meal. For me it is perfect. It gives me just enough satisfaction so that I am no longer starving without giving me that full feeling. Now I get to enjoy the main course and taste every savory flavor within the actual meal. As a worship leader, your job is to prepare the people for the word of God. You create an atmosphere where people can hear from God and receive of His word. You are the worshipper not the preacher. Preaching during your worship set is like trying to feed people a meal before their meal. By the time the preacher gets up to speak, people are still chewing on what you preached to them. And quite possibly, they do not have the capacity to digest *more* food. Trust that whomever the Lord has called to speak after you has the Word that God wants them to say. Just worship. Just sing. Just lead the songs. If you have a word, share it with your team before or after the service. Even then, it should be in conjunction with what has been preached and not in competition with it. The worship and the word go hand in hand; if you put them together, you will create explosive transformation in the lives of the congregation.

TWEET 62

#DEARWORSHIPLEADER IF THE SENIOR PASTOR DOESN'T LIKE IT, THEN DON'T DO IT. IF YOU WON'T FOLLOW THEIR LEAD, YOU WON'T FOLLOW GOD'S EITHER.

My children have a habit of trying to divide their mom and me. They will ask one of us for something and, if that parent says no, then they will go and ask the other parent in hopes of getting a yes. Whenever they ask me for something the first question I ask is, "Did you ask your mother?" The second question I ask is, "What did she say?" If she said no then I'm going to say no because we cannot let our children divide us. The senior pastor is the "parent" of the church. Before you make a move, you should discuss it with them first. It is their church, not yours. Talk to them about song selection, style of dress, placement of singers, who gets to lead, what is their vision and every other possible question you can think of. You are there to push their vision, not yours. And if you ever find you are doing something that the senior pastor does not like then you must abort it. Unfortunately, too many worship leaders take matters into their own hands and do things that are not in the vision of the pastor. A common response to this from worship leaders is that they felt led by God. One of my favorite preachers tells his team, "If you want to feel "led", go to the junk yard, find some *lead*, and feel it so that you don't have to feel "led" on the stage." You cannot circumvent your pastor by going to God. That is trying to divide God and your pastor. The truth is they talk a lot more than you think they do. And God put that person in the position they are in because that is the person He gave the vision to. So support your pastor, walk in agreement with your church, and see the blessing of the Lord come upon your ministry.

TWEET 63

#DEARWORSHIPLEADER SOMETIMES OUR SEASON IS UP. EMBRACE IT. GOD HAS SO MUCH MORE IN STORE FOR US.

God takes us from faith to faith and from glory to glory. There are levels in faith and there are levels of glory. Often, when God takes you to a new level of faith He brings you through a new season of life. God will push you into the next level of glory by taking you out of your comfort and into a new assignment. God is not the author of confusion, but He can be the author of frustration. God will allow us to be so uncomfortable in an environment that it forces us to seek His face for wisdom and understanding. I have been through seasons in my life where rehearsals stopped being fun, picking songs became tedious work, and leading worship was like punching in to work. It felt more as if I was doing a job than engaging in ministry. I was on autopilot. I blamed it on my Pastor, my church, my worship team, and anything else I could think. However, the truth is that my season had changed. God was shifting me to a new assignment and I was not aware of it. The ceiling I once looked up at had now become the floor. And God was taking me higher. You will always be a worship leader. However, you may not always be a worship leader in the same way you are right now. Your location can change. Your role can change. Maybe your assignment now is to do more teaching and training of the next generation. Whatever it is, seek the face of God. Be married to Christ not to worship leading. Do not be so attached to an old assignment that you miss a new instruction. Seek the Lord for your next season in ministry.

TWEET 64

#DEARWORSHIPLEADER YOU MUST TRAIN SOMEONE YOUNGER TO DO WHAT YOU DO. YOUR PASTOR AND YOUR CHURCH WILL THANK YOU!

Part of our responsibility as worship leaders is to identify, recruit, and train new worship leaders to do what we do. If you are intimidated by newer and younger worship leaders, then you have an unhealthy attachment to your assignment. If you cannot train the next generation because you fear that they are going to replace you, then there is something broken within you that has to be brought to wholeness. The kingdom is bigger than you are. If we are going to expand God's work on the earth then we must make disciples of all nations. Your ability to disciple other worship leaders is more valuable than your ability to sing. When you sing you bless people for a moment. When you disciple others you bless people for a lifetime. Because the person you disciple, will disciple someone else who will go and disciple someone else, and your work will continue. I know what it feels like to be the young hot shot who became the old pop tart. However, the best way to stay relevant, fresh, and creative is to constantly pour into the next generation. You need a successor and they need your wisdom. The lessons you have learned and battles you have fought should not die with you. It should be shared and explained to someone else. That is how the kingdom works. That is how the church continues to grow. That is how your legacy will live on when you are done. Developing yourself can make you a leader. Making disciples of others will make you a legend. #BeLegendary

TWEET 65

#DEARWORSHIPLEADER THIS IS NOT A COMPETITION. IF GOD CALLED YOU THEN HE QUALIFIED YOU. SO JUST BE YOU!

One of my favorite quotes in all the world is "Everyone is a genius. But if you judge a fish by its ability to climb trees it will spend the rest of its life thinking that it's dumb." Too many people compare themselves to others. We are all called by God and qualified for this position. Each of us bring something unique to worship leading. Some of us are phenomenal singers. Some possess incredible musicianship. Some have great energy, while others are laid back. Each of us bring our own story, personality, and anointing to worship leading. Never let the way someone else does it make you feel inferior. Your voice is important. Your gift is unique. God called you for a reason. He did not choose you because you reminded Him of someone else. He chose you because of what He placed in you from the time you were born. Whether you are short or tall, black or white, conservative or contemporary, outgoing or introverted, you have been called, anointed and appointed to lead people in worship. Do not be a fish trying to climb trees. Do what you were created to do. God has called you for such a time as this.

Made in the USA
Middletown, DE
21 July 2018